BEING

Happy

"*Anyone that is not happy, does not claim their birthright.*"

Theron Q Dumont

BEING

Happy

10 Keys to Unlock Overflowing Joy

In Everyday Living

Janice Almond

Los Angeles   Washington, D C

Copyright © 2018 Janice Almond

BEING HAPPY: 10 Keys to Unlock Overflowing Joy in Everyday Living

Published by ZION Publishing House

Los Angeles & Washington, D. C.

www.zionpublishinghouse.com

ISBN: 978-0-9983845-5-9

Cover by Chantal Hayes Designs

All rights reserved. The author guarantees all contents are original and do not infringe upon the legal rights of any other person or work. No part of this book may be reproduced, distributed, or transmitted in any form or by any means –electronic, mechanical, digital, photocopy, recording, or any other—except for brief quotations in printed reviews, without the prior written permission of the publisher.

    Unless otherwise indicated, Bible quotations are taken from the *New King James Version*, (NKJV). Copyright © by Thomas Nelson, 1982. Used by permission. All rights reserved.

    Other version used is: *New International Version,* (NIV). Copyright © by Zondervan Publishing House, 1984. Used by permission. All rights reserved.

Printed in the United States of America

Dedication:

I dedicate this third and final book in my BEING GRATEFUL series to God, my Savior. It is because of Him, I have been able to complete this task.

KEYS:

Acknowledgements: ix
Foreword: xi
Introduction: xiii
KEY #1 *Be Yourself* 1
KEY #2 *Energize Your Soul* 9
KEY #3 *Incite Joy* 17
KEY #4 *Nourish Your Mind* 25
KEY #5 *Give of Yourself* 33
KEY #6 *Have Expectation* 39
Key #7 *Appreciate Life* 47
KEY #8 *Permit Mistakes* 55
KEY #9 *Purpose to Live* 61
Key #10 *Yearn for the Best* 69
ABOUT THE AUTHOR 81
About ZION Publishing House 83

Acknowledgements:

To my family, the Almonds. You have been the source of my joy and the reason I write. I have garnered ideas and stories just from being around you-all. May God continually bless all that your hands find to do.

                In His great love,

                    Janice

x

Foreword:

Almost twenty-five years ago I met Janice and her husband, David. My wife's first words to me after our initial meeting with this amazing couple were, "Janice sure has a unique laugh, doesn't she?" "Yes she does," I responded, "She certainly does. It's probably because she's such a unique person." Since that time I've learned the truth of my response.

Because I worked with David at the Los Angeles Mission and witnessed first-hand his strength and godly character, I have come to understand the source of support and encouragement that reinforce the continued development of her own godly character. Having had the opportunity to be in their home and to see her motherly love in action convinced me that Janice was not only a unique individual, but that she is indeed a special person with a special relationship with our Lord.

Janice's writing style is simple and direct. The words she weaves together to form the truths and principles that she wants to communicate to her readers are proof of God's influence in her life. A life of prayer, faith, and obedience to the leading of the Holy Spirit has given her wisdom beyond her years. I've been reading her newsletters for as long as I can remember and look forward to the truth and encouragement she shares in every issue.

If you want to be uplifted and encouraged, you will find her work like medicine for your soul. Because of God's blessing upon Janice, she is a blessing to all who read and meditate on the truths she shares. What a privilege and honor it is to be able to call her and David our friends. My wife and I both look forward to our times of fellowship with the Almonds and are proud to tell others of the "special" bond we share with them. Even now I can hear the sound of her laughter echoing through the recesses of my mind... happy, encouraging, loving, and filled with the truth and wisdom her gracious God has built into this special saint.

Read her book and be ready to be blessed.

Ron Gonzales, CEO

Innovative Learning Systems

Introduction:

If you want to be happy, you can be! This begins our third journey in our BEING GRATEFUL series. The first book, *BEING GRATEFUL: How to Open the Door to a More Fulfilled & Abundant Life in 13 Easy Steps*, gave you an "attitude of gratitude." The second book, *BEING DETERMINED: How to be Relentless in Pursuing Your Dreams in 15 Simple Ways*, helped you with your ability to have more determination to reach your dreams. Now, *BEING HAPPY: 10 Keys to Unlock Overflowing Joy in Everyday Living* will take you a step further as you travel the path to a happiness that lasts.

One thing we have learned, our thoughts control our ability to be grateful and determined. Thoughts also determine our level of happiness. We need to constantly realize we are in control of our minds. Though, at times, being happy may be a struggle—you can do it! You can choose to be happy. Everything is NOT all bad.

The *10 Keys* we will experience in this book are:

*Be Yourself

*Energize Your Soul

*Incite Joy

*Nourish Your Mind

*Give of Yourself

*Have Expectation

*Appreciate Life

*Permit Mistakes

*Purpose to Live

*Yearn for the Best

As you read through these pages, you will discover that happiness is not elusive. You **can** unlock overflowing joy. Joy matters and depends on your attitude and how you think. *As you think, so you are.* You must choose to live for today. Not for yesterday and not for tomorrow. This "happy" journey is one you must savor. Do not let another day go by while you wallow in sadness, grief, or regret. I urge you to take these "keys" and unlock a joy that overflows.

Key #1   Be Yourself

"Be yourself because an original is worth more than a copy."

author unknown

Choose to be yourself. Why would you want to be anyone else? True happiness will come only if you are you! Don't try being like someone else. You are you. You are unique. Our Creator designed you that way. All you do is trust the process. Don't let another day go by trying to be who or what you're not.

Being yourself will lead to many more opportunities in life than being a "fake" will. Unhappiness will be your lot in life if you are constantly trying to conform to others or live up to other's expectations of who or what you should be. Plus, it's tiring and confusing trying to always think that you have to please others or compare yourself to others.

Think about this. You are the most content when you *are* yourself and can be yourself. Truth be told, the unhappiest people are those who do not like themselves. You may be asking yourself, "How can I be happy?" "How can I like myself?" You can be grateful because you are not an accident, and you are here for a reason. Read the Psalm below:

Psalm 139:13-15
New King James Version (NKJV)

¹³ For You formed my inward parts;
You covered me in my mother's womb.
¹⁴ I will praise You, for I am
*fearfully **and** wonderfully made;*
Marvelous are Your works,
*And **that** my soul knows very well.*
¹⁵ My frame was not hidden from You,
When I was made in secret,
***And** skillfully wrought in the lowest parts of the earth.*

You have a reason for happiness simply because you are *fearfully and wonderfully made*. Stop **now** and meditate on that for a moment. Contemplate this quote, "You will find peace not by rearranging the circumstances of your life, but by realizing who you are at the deepest level." Eckhart Tolle, author of *The Power of Now: A Guide to Spiritual Enlightenment*

Jot down one thing in your favor:

_____

Focus, Concentrate, and Be happy for that. Accept peace.
Now, think of some more things that are unique about you. Don't be shy or think you are being conceited.

It is time to start thinking about how wonderful you really are. Needless to say, if you can't or don't see anything unique about you, how will you "be you"? You won't be able to be yourself if you don't know who you are.

Do Now: MAKE A LIST!

Title it:

"My Uniqueness" Think of at least ten things unique to you. As you make this list, you will begin to get more of a handle on who you are. What is unique and wonderful about you? What is it that only you can do? What do you do best? What is your image of yourself? Think also about what identifies you and drives you.

It is easy to compare yourself and your situation with that of others. You are you. You are not your neighbor, your best friend, your sister, your mother, or anyone else. If you are comparing yourself to someone else, stop it, NOW! Be you!
Be authentic and true to yourself, and you will be a catalyst to allow others to be authentic and true to themselves. We could start a chain reaction. Perhaps we could carry signs that read "Be Yourself"!

Something unique to me is my laugh. Those who know me well know that my laugh is very loud and highly contagious! No matter where I go or where I've been, there is always the same question, "Janice, were you at such'n such place at such'n such time? I most always was. You see the person didn't actually see me, but they heard my laugh! In fact, my laugh is so unique, I had thought about making a "laugh box".

One instance in my marriage, my husband and I were sitting on the balcony of the Pantages Theatre in Hollywood. We were watching a movie called, *Gator*. There was a funny scene, and I let "it" loose. My laugh, that is. Right then, people sitting down below turned around and started pointing up at me. My husband started crouching down in his seat so as not to be seen with me.

Although I am older now, my laugh hasn't changed. It remains a part of me and is a part of my uniqueness.

If you are having a hard time thinking about some unique things about yourself, maybe you feel that you are lacking in too many areas. Read these words out loud:

Today, I am enough. I am smart enough. Wise enough. Clever enough.

Resourceful enough. Able enough. Confident enough.

I am connected to enough people to accomplish my heart's desire.

I have enough ideas to pull off magic and miracles. Enough is all I need.

Enough is what I have. I have more than enough.

You feel better about yourself now? Truth be told, saying good and positive things about yourself—affirmations, have been known to work.

The quote above said you would find peace by knowing who you are at the "deepest level." To be yourself, you will need to find peace. A peaceful heart is a happy heart. Be true to yourself. You cannot be true to yourself by allowing other people, incidents, or events change you or cause you unhappiness. *Like* who you are.

Remember the story, *The Ugly Duckling*? *The Ugly Duckling*, originally published in 1843 by Hans Christian Anderson, a Danish poet and author, is a story about an ugly bird (duck). The duck thought himself ugly and doomed to a life of failure and misery. In the end, he learns that he is a swan, full of beauty and elegance—the most beautiful bird of all.

This is a great fairy tale and has a great theme. Realize who you are. You must like yourself. Similar to the "ugly duckling," your life will be full of misery if you can't understand or don't realize your beauty. You can be yourself only when you value yourself. Just the mere fact that you are a creation of God and made in His image, (see *Psalm 139*) gives you beauty and value. It is not what people may say about you (in a negative way) that is true, but what God says about you.

Start telling yourself you are unique and original. Stop putting yourself down. Don't compare yourself with others. Stop listening to others' negativity. Be who God created you to be. Challenge yourself to be the best you, YOU can be! "To be yourself in a world that is constantly trying to make you something else is the greatest accomplishment." Ralph Waldo Emerson, American essayist, lecturer, and poet, (1803-1882).

As a youngster, I had to learn to like myself and be myself. Being super skinny made me self-conscious. I constantly felt that I had to prove myself and be better than others both physically and intellectually. Not only were my arms and legs like rails, my right foot turned inward when I stood and walked. Even to this day, my right foot turns inward.

Because of my small size during elementary school, I was determined to beat everyone in tether-ball. No one thought my skinny arms could hit the ball around the pole, much less defeat them in the process.

As it turns out, I was good at telling myself I could beat everyone. And that, I did!

Take this moment to challenge yourself to like yourself, and most importantly, to be yourself!

Say aloud:

"I like myself"

"I am enough"

"I am unique"

"I am fearfully and wonderfully made"

Being yourself will make you more confident. Confidence will enable you to approach life boldly and with more daring and fearlessness to overcome life's issues and setbacks. Being yourself will make you happier. By accepting you have value, your life's journey toward success will be more assured. As we begin this journey toward a greater sense of happiness, remember you DO have enough and you ARE enough.

Here is a list of five I AM statements: Say, **I AM**...

1. A child of God (*Romans 8:16*)

2. Led by the Spirit of God (*Romans 8:14*)

3. Strong in the Lord and in the power of His might (*Ephesians 6:10*)

4. Doing all things through Christ who strengthens me (*Philippians 4:13*)

5. More than a conqueror (*Romans 8:37*)

Look them up, read them daily, learn them, and meditate on them frequently. What you say will help reinforce what you think. See yourself differently by what you tell yourself. Examine your inner thoughts.

WHY I MUST BE MYSELF: List as many reasons as you can. **Do this NOW**.

COMPLETE THIS SENTENCE: Actions that I can take to *be myself* are…

Key #2 Energize Your Soul

"You cannot have a positive life and a negative mind."

Joyce Meyer

Choose to energize your soul. What does it mean to "energize" your soul? Energize means to "give vitality and enthusiasm to," "supply energy to." Why would you want to energize your soul? If you do not energize your soul, your life will have no spark. Your life will literally be without "life." You will just be existing. Who wants to live a life like that? Who wants to just exist? A dead life is no life! That is an oxymoron.

Giving your life vitality and energy is a daily process that can take many forms; from exercising, to reading, to meditating, to praying, and helping others. Whatever excites you and brings joy into your atmosphere is something you must cultivate. Just like putting seeds in the ground, plant that which you want to grow and have a harvest.

"A merry heart doeth good like a medicine, but a broken spirit drieth the bones." **Proverbs 17:22** (NKJV). To energize your soul, pick something that facilitates enthusiasm for you and gives you a "lift!" Think about what that could be. Don't wait for another day to begin.

Having energy and an enthusiastic mindset will push you to excel. Jim Rohn, entrepreneur, author, and motivational speaker, (1930-2009) once said, "Happiness is not something you postpone for the future; it is something you design for the moment."

One of the best ways to energize your soul is to be a positive person. Motivation for living can come from being positive. Positivity gives you vitality, energy, and enthusiasm. It gives you a lift! In my first book, *BEING GRATEFUL: How to Open the Door to a More Fulfilled & Abundant Life in 13 Easy Steps*, in Step#8 Always Be Positive, I talk about "Positivity" and "Negativity." I call them boxers in a ring and how you must fight *tooth & nail* for "Positivity" to win.

Do NOW: Take the time and write down a list of the positive things in your life. Read them when you start to think negative thoughts. It is difficult to be unhappy when you have and maintain vitality for life and are positive. Remember, what you think about yourself is important.

Take me for instance. Here is a partial list of **some** of the positive things in my life. I like to call them *blessings*:

1. I am a Christian, a devoted follower of Jesus Christ.
2. I have been married to my husband for forty-two years.

3. Both of my parents are alive. My dad is eighty-seven, and my mom is eighty-four.
4. I have four wonderful children and nine "pretty fabulous" grandchildren.
5. My health and mind are good.

I could have added more, but I just want to whet your appetite about starting your own list and to let you realize that you can start somewhere.

Thinking negatively will "zap" your energy and deplete your soul. Daily, you are designing your moments. Simply concentrate on what you're thinking about. If what you are thinking about isn't lifting your spirits, stop thinking it!

Another way to energize your soul is with music. What kind of music do you like? Put on some inspirational tunes and sing or hum along! It doesn't matter if you can't carry a tune. Make a joyful noise! There are so many varieties. Uplifting music can cause harmony within your spirit, can stir up a cheerful attitude, and put you in the right frame of mind. For example, I love gospel music, contemporary Christian music, and country music! There's nothing quite like music to lift my spirits. I also enjoy church hymns and orchestra music. Try it! Let music bless your soul.

To energize your soul, try meditating or praying. Get in a quiet spot, close your eyes, and think and reflect on positive and uplifting moments in your life. Take deep breaths and relax all over each part of your body. Now, empty your mind of all thoughts and just **be**. Be thankful and appreciative of what you have. You have life. You have this moment. For these reasons alone, you are blessed. Allow your soul to be energized today and tomorrow and for as long as you have breath.

Hear what John Wooden said, (1910-2010), American basketball player and head coach at the University of California at Los Angeles, UCLA. "Things turn out best for the people who make the best of the way things turn out." How true this is. I have often heard it said that your attitude determines your altitude. If you want to live higher, lift your soul higher. See every day as a day to experience something good. Be energized no matter what is happening in your life or in the world.

Let nature energize you. Think about the wonder of the world around you. Last week, we went to Sequoia National Park. That is a wonder! Those redwood trees are a magnificent sight to behold. Just being surrounded by those trees does magic to your spirit! The park was filled with so many wonderful sights and smells. I could hardly believe my eyes! I couldn't believe that it took me so long to finally go see for myself. I marveled at God's masterpiece.

Surrounding yourself with the presence of serenity will do wonders for your soul. Go outside. Look at the sky, the sun, the clouds, the trees, the birds, feel the rain, smell the flowers, touch the grass. Be in awe of the magnificence of the stars, the moon, the darkness, the sounds, the movement in the sky. You will feel a sense of contentment. Enjoy these free gifts we have been given.

My soul is also energized when I exercise. No matter where I am in any city or state, I can exercise. Exercising helps lower anxiety and decreases depression. In fact, exercising in nature is a double bonus. If you need an emotional recharging, go out and spend awhile in nature. Since I have a bad left knee, I can't run too much, so I walk fast. I make my way around while being thankful I can move and have the activity of my limbs.

Perhaps you are down and can't move your soul because of unforgiveness abiding in your heart. This is something you have to let go of! There is no option. Unforgiveness kills your soul. It drains your soul of vitality and energy. Forgiveness is a choice. It's not easy by any means and may even take a few unsuccessful attempts until we can emotionally forgive. Your pain will not completely leave your heart until you completely forgive that person or that situation.

Really, it takes an act of your will. It takes not bringing the situation, event, or hurt up again. It takes releasing that person of their debt. I will admit some situations will affect your sense of being happy. It can be a struggle. But, this is when you have to appropriate some "will power"! You have to choose happiness now.

Think of someone you know who is energized. More often than not, they act energized because they feel energized. He or she is excited about life and living. "Catch on fire with enthusiasm and people will come for miles to watch you burn."—John Wesley, (1703-1791) the founder of Methodism.

You can energize your soul if you…
Stop! Look! Listen!

Stop! Stop this minute. No matter what you're doing, stop **NOW** and take a deep breath. As you're taking this breath, silently count to ten. Take another one. How often do you just "stop" during the day and take a minute off? Take a Power Minute! Your mind needs a rest. Your body does, too. Slow them both down. Stop the *rat race* for a minute.

Look! Look around you. What do you see? Do you see or notice anything different that you haven't noticed before? Pick something that you haven't paid much attention to in the past. You will find it amazing how much you miss "looking at" because of so many other things demanding your attention. Your time is slipping by, and you're missing much of life by not actually being open to looking at what you don't see or haven't seen in the past. It could be the smile of a child, the glow of the moon, the colors in the sky, or the fluttering of a butterfly. Decide today to look up and look around.

Listen! What do you hear? What have you missed hearing simply because you don't take the time to really hear? Every day you miss something vitally important for your well-being because you can't, don't, or won't hear it. We are all guilty. We have to learn to train our ears to become more perceptive to the sounds, happenings, and people around us. Just driving around town you may notice that people do not always listen. I find myself stunned when the sound of an ambulance is ignored, and cars do not move to the side of the street or even slow down. If you are too busy to hear the sound of an emergency, you are simply way too busy.

Tomorrow, practice this: *stopping*, *looking*, and *listening*. Start right this moment to energize your entire being and start an enthusiastic fire that people want to watch burn. To do that, you must have zeal. You have to put forth effort. If you want to feel energized, you have to act energized. You know what they say, "Act as IF"! Being energized will also help you to be able to do the next key step, *Incite Joy*. Remember the quote at the beginning of this chapter? You can't live or have a positive life with a negative mind. Think about it. We will talk more about the mind in *Key #4 Nourish Your Mind*.

WHY I MUST ENERGIZE MY SOUL: List your reasons **Now**.

COMPLETE THIS SENTENCE: Actions I can take to *energize my soul* are…

Key #3   Incite Joy

"Wake up early. Life is short. What if today is the last night of my life, so enjoy life to the full."

Robin Sharma

Choose to incite joy. Why? Life is short! You can't wait to enjoy life as life passes quickly. In fact, you might not wake up tomorrow. Listen to what the scripture says in **Proverbs 15:13**, *"A merry heart makes a cheerful countenance, but by sorrow of the heart the spirit is broken."* (NKJV) WOW! Having joy or a merry heart is a great thing. Looking happy is a great thing! Cheerfulness will give you joy and help you smile. Joy is contagious! You can have and cultivate joy if you want. Be intentional. Develop some "will power" as I mentioned in the last chapter.

One thing to remember is anxiety will not help you discover and live with joy. Anxiety is the enemy of joy. This is exactly why you have to "incite" joy. Incite means to *stir up, whip up, encourage, kindle, excite, stimulate, arouse* or *provoke*. You might wake up in the morning and not automatically feel joy or feel like rejoicing. Bad news has a way of diminishing our sense of joy. This is when you must arouse and whip "it" up, similar to arousing yourself out of sleep.

This attitude of cheerfulness or being cheerful can literally change your whole life because it changes your perspective. You can either see the glass as "half-empty" or "half-full". As you stimulate yourself, your steps become lighter, and your life atmosphere changes. Choose today to celebrate something in your life. It could be an accomplishment, a blessing, or, yes, even a setback because all of life benefits you in developing your character.

Tell yourself that today is the day you finally quit worrying. What has worry ever done for you? Think about it. Write down how it has helped you. I bet worry has only paralyzed you in some emotional way. I submit to you that although we have a tendency to worry, it is really a waste of time. It is useless. "There is nothing that wastes the body like worry, and one who has any faith in God should be ashamed to worry about anything," Mahatma Gandhi- Indian Civil Rights leader, (1869-1948).

John Haggai said, "Worry is an intrusion into God's providence." You can't worry and be happy at the same time. Worry will sap your joy! Get rid of your sorrow and enjoy your life to the full. Let God handle what you can't. I heard someone say once, *Pray and let God worry*. If you are worrying, stop it this minute! Keep your body from wasting away.

You can have joy if you are thankful. Cultivate joy today! Joy is enthusiasm. Try hugging someone. See how just this simple act of a hug brings joy. There was a story I heard on the radio. It went something like this:

A young man was a passenger on a commuter train. Everyone could see that he was "freaking out!" He was hollering and screaming about how terrible his life was at the top of his lungs. A seventy-year-old woman got up out of her seat, went over to this young man, and simply touched him. Can you imagine this? Simply a touch. Whatever this touch was, was all that this man needed. The story goes on to say, he immediately calmed down. Think of that. Incredible! This woman simply passed her inner "joy" and "peace" onto this complete stranger.

After her touch, he stopped. Remember this story and share your inner joy and peace with those around you. People desperately need it. Think about who you can touch emotionally today. You know someone who needs a hug. You are alive to encourage and inspire someone today. Even a "good word" in passing, can do the trick.

You can still choose to be happy in spite of the bad happening around you, if you concentrate on what is good. Yes, there are some things I would rather not have to deal with, but that is all a part of life. Instead, I choose to focus on the "good report" right now. I just have to keep my joy anyway. You have to do this, too. Everything is not ALL bad. Focus on being thankful and focus on the good.

Here is what **Philippians 4:8** (Amplified version) says,

"Finally, believers, whatever is true, whatever is honorable and worthy of respect, whatever is right and confirmed by

God's word, whatever is pure and wholesome, whatever is lovely and brings peace, whatever is admirable and of good repute; if there is any excellence, if there is anything worthy of praise, think continually on these things."

Say you will have joy, and you will! I am a firm believer is saying what you want and how you want to feel. There is power in your words. If you have never done this, said a declaration or affirmation about something needed in your life, **do it now**!

Thankfulness will incite joy. Write down the things you are thankful for:

One thing I will say is: Don't let anyone or anything ever steal your joy. It isn't worth it. You need joy to live. The scriptures say in **Nehemiah 8:10**, "*, for the joy of the Lord is your strength.*" (NKJV) Sometimes it is a battle to keep your joy. Throughout the day, you may find a myriad of people, happenings, or events that can be a downer and that can bring you down. I am in the midst of a personal family situation right now that is a downer. So, I remember and heed the above scripture.

You can't live in a state of depression. It's impossible. You can try to live a life depressed, but you won't succeed. I have tried it. That's why I daily choose joy. Robin Sharma, a Canadian writer and leadership speaker, has also said, "We don't laugh because we are happy. We are happy because we laugh."

Try laughing! Share your excitement, hold your head up, and keep your heart happy. Bring a smile to someone today. Sincerely praise someone today. You are passing through this way but once, remember to spread the joy, and see them light up!

Do NOW: If possible, get up NOW and walk, jog, bike, or drive to a secluded spot. Hopefully, you can find a scenic area and simply commune with nature. Sit down or lie down and "breathe-in" the sights and smells. Don't rush this time. Spend fifteen-thirty minutes if you can. Let this time recharge you as you marvel in God's creation. Bring a smile to your heart and your spirit!

The woods, lakes, and oceans can conjure up thoughts of joy and happiness. One of my many pleasures is going to the beaches in Southern California. What a serenity this brings to my spirit! Just sitting and watching the waves or walking along the shoreline is a source of tranquility and peace. Something so easy and so simple incites joy. "It's not how much we have, but how much we enjoy, that makes happiness." Charles Spurgeon, former theologian and English Particular Baptist preacher (1834-1892).

Find out what gives you joy and what you enjoy and do that. Maybe, reading comic books. Maybe, watching old black and white movies. Maybe, it's painting. It might be singing or playing a musical instrument. Maybe, shopping or hanging out with others. For me, it's spending time with my grandchildren. **Write down some things**. Now, make time for these. It does absolutely no good to write anything down and then never do any of it.

You might be feeling that you can't incite any joy because of having made too many mistakes in the past. I can relate to that feeling. We all have the tendency to cry over spilt milk. But those feelings and thoughts only bring sorrow and not any happiness. Let me make a suggestion, no longer cry over your failures. Our shortcomings are many. In this chapter and in this book, we are focusing on JOY-*BEING HAPPY*. Joy despite our shortcomings. That's how it works.

Quit wasting time. Seize your moments today! I wake up in the morning and pray my way to joy. I stir up praise and arouse my spirit by singing. I don't rush this time. I know I need joy to live my everyday life. Without joy, I have no strength. Without joy, you cannot be strong. Quit worrying. Be joyful and laugh! Here's a suggestion, tonight, before you go to bed, go outside and look at the stars and say, "Wow"! Enjoy life to the full! You will have too many regrets if you don't.

WHY I MUST INCITE JOY: Come up with as many reasons as you can think of. Write them down **now**.

COMPLETE THIS SENTENCE: Actions I can take to *incite joy* are...

Key #4   Nourish Your Mind

"For as he thinks in his heart, so is he."

Proverbs 23:7

C**hoose to nourish your mind**. What are you thinking about right now? Is it nourishing your mind or diminishing it? Nourishing your mind is important because you must control what you think about. Thinking haphazardly will not work. Thinking trashy thoughts will get you trashy results. Sometimes, you have to encourage yourself no matter how you feel. This is a deliberate and determined process.

Ask yourself these questions:

>   **What am I reading?*
>
>   **What am I watching?*
>
>   **What am I believing?*
>
>   **What am I hearing?*
>
>   **What am I saying?*

Nourishing your mind is like controlling a thermostat. What you allow into your mind will either "up" your happiness or lower it. This is no small matter.

What you read, what you watch, what you believe, what you hear, and what words come out of your mouth will determine your level of happiness. Whatever you ingest into your life, good or bad, works its way into your heart, affecting your thoughts. You can rise high or sink low based on what you do daily. It depends on how and what you feed your mind. Your mouth speaks what your heart holds. **Matthew 12:34b** "……. *for out of the abundance of the heart the mouth speaks."* (NKJV)

You nourish your mind by building it up and strengthening it. The Bible says, *"All things are possible to him who believes."* **Mark 9:23** (NKJV). I have this on my car license plate MARK923. Why is it important to believe in something? What you believe in comes to pass. You can overcome obstacles and create a joyful life by thinking joy-filled thoughts.

Never take your thoughts lightly. Prepare to win by what you're thinking. You have to use your imagination to be able to "see." Get some "happy" mental imagery. You can do this by reading a *Psalm* a day. To be happy, you must tell your mind you are happy! Seems easy, doesn't it? Stop right now and tell yourself, "I am happy!" How about you do this simple exercise daily. Wake up in the morning, go to a mirror, look at your face, and say it out loud. Here is a good Psalm for you.

> *Make a joyful shout to the Lord, all you lands! Serve the Lord with gladness. Come before His presence with singing. Know that the Lord, He is God. It is He who has made us and not we ourselves. We are His people and the sheep of His*

pasture. Enter into His gates with thanksgiving, and into His courts with praise. Be thankful to Him, and bless His name. For the Lord is good. His mercy is everlasting. And His truth endures to all generations.

Psalm 100 (NKJV)

It will take constant deliberation and determination to keep your mind nourished. Guarding your mind and your heart takes a twenty-four-hour vigilance. Think of everything you can do to maintain the discipline it will take to keep your thermostat high. Be diligent on what you read, watch, hear, and speak. Only watch T.V. programs that help in this endeavor. Only read magazines, papers, and books that help you along this process. Only hear words and music that help sustain an "uplifting" outlook, and only speak what promotes thankfulness.

Mahatma Gandhi also said this, "A man is but the product of his thoughts. What he thinks, he becomes." How does this happen? It happens because what is in your mind feeds into your spirit and determines your life's outcome. You can *think* yourself unhappy. You can *think* yourself happy. Eckhart Tolle, author, also said, "The primary cause of unhappiness is never the situation but your thoughts about it." Could this be any clearer?

You must, from this day forward, truly think about what you think about. It will determine everything! Your thinking will determine who or what you're going to be, what you're going to have and do, how you're going to live your life, and where you're going to end up. It is a big deal. Instead of thinking small, think great!

I remember as a junior high student, having the opportunity to try out for the city's girls' softball team. I was super elated about this because my best friend was also trying out. I knew she would make it because she had skills. On the other hand, my skills were not the greatest. I was also scared. I almost backed out!

I tried out and made the team. Although not the most skilled player, I kept improving with every game. Although scared, I kept pushing myself to do my best. In fact, after a few games, I was moved from right field to short stop. This was a major feat. With each game, my hitting also improved. I was a proud team member. Instead of telling myself I couldn't do it, I told myself I could, and I did!

If you don't nourish your mind and continue "stinking thinking", you will limit your life possibilities. You must think "you can" in order "to." You must be totally committed to rejecting any and all negativity and not waver. What you do with your mind is crucial, not a laughing matter. You will do what your mind tells you to do.

In the last chapter, Key #3 *Incite Joy,* you read the Bible verse, **Philippians 4:8**. If your thoughts don't fit into any one of these categories, don't allow them. Refuse unnourishing and negative thoughts. Say this word three times: Discipline! Discipline! Discipline! This is all it takes.

You may think you have it bad. Is your situation worse than Corrie Ten Boom's, for example? Corrie ten Boom, (1892-1983) published her autobiography, *The Hiding Place*, in 1971—a story of her and her family's horrific ordeal during the Nazi Holocaust. Corrie's story is truly remarkable! During WWII, Corrie and her family became a part of the Dutch underground, turning their home into a hiding place for Jews and others who were being hunted by the Nazis.

The Ten Boom family was arrested and sent to a prison. Much of the family was released, some died, but Corrie and her sister, Betsie, were tried for their actions and sent to a political concentration camp.

Miraculously, Corrie survived this atrocity, though sadly her sister did not. Because of a "clerical error," Corrie was released from Ravensbrück concentration camp just a week before all the other women were killed. She and her family demonstrated the "power to stand." After her release, Corrie continued to spread the hope and love of Jesus. When she was fifty-three, she began a ministry traveling to more than sixty countries over the course of the next thirty-two years. WOW!

How did Corrie keep her sanity? By trusting in God. She said this, "God does not have problems, only plans. When a train goes through a tunnel, and it gets dark, you don't throw away your ticket and jump off. You sit still and trust the engineer." She kept hope alive even in that totally dark and horrendous situation. Corrie was able to survive because she kept her mind right. She often recalled something her sister said while they were at the camp together, "There is no pit so deep that God's love is not deeper still."

Listen to this quote from John Wooden, American basketball coach, (1910-2010), "There are many things that are essential to arriving at true peace of mind, and one of the most important is faith, which cannot be acquired without prayer." Prayer. Do you pray? This is one of the best ways to let God's thoughts nourish you. You are responsible for your state of mind. You have to control your mind.

Repeat daily: *I am going to choose my own thoughts and hold them as long as I choose. I am going to shut out all thoughts that weaken or interfere, that make me timid. My will is as strong as anyone else's.* –from *The Power of Concentration* by Theron Q. Dumont.

Whether you want to believe it or not, there is a battle for your mind! This is a constant, every second battle. Your mind and how you nourish it is the key. Where is your faith? The most important thing to keep in mind is to not allow your mind to become stagnant. You know how much "gunk" there is in stagnant water? Now, translate that image to your mind. Perhaps, it is time for a mind cleansing.
Tell yourself what you **"will!"** These are called "affirmations."

Do NOW: Tell yourself something affirming. Say it out loud! You want your mind and spirit to hear it. Suggestions:

1. "I can do all things through Christ Who strengthens me!"
2. "I am making it!"
3. "I am thankful!"

I have an *I AM* sheet. It has a list of 40 phrases dealing with Christian principles. You can compile a similar sheet of your values and beliefs. The main thing is to have some positive, affirming words that you can look at and say daily to keep you focused on forward progress. Nourishing your mind will give you more peace and help eliminate stress. Keep singing! Nourish your mind with joy and praise. Remember, you become what you think you are.

WHY I MUST NOURISH MY MIND: List as many reasons as you can.

COMPLETE THIS SENTENCE: Actions that I can take to *nourish my mind* are...

Key #5   Give of Yourself

"To know that even one life has breathed easier because you have lived. This is to have succeeded!"

Ralph Waldo Emerson

Choose to give of yourself. Why do you want to be a giver? Stingy people aren't happy. Look at Mr. Scrooge, the character in *A Christmas Carol*. He was very stingy and extremely unhappy. To him, Christmas was "bah-humbug!" It wasn't until he learned to give of himself and put others first, that he became a happy, joyful person. You must do that, too. In order for you to become a happy, joyful person, you can't just think of yourself. You can't be stingy. The saying, "*it is more blessed to give than to receive,*" is found in **Acts 20:35** (NKJV).

How many ways can you give of yourself? You can give a word of encouragement. You can give a word of praise. How many of us need that? You can give a smile, a hug, a wave, and more. You can give of your time. You can give of your money. You can give of yourself by being a friend. We all need a friend. You can reach out to others. You might be surprised how a seemingly small gesture can lift someone's spirits and perhaps change his or her life for the better.

Think about what you can give. Think about how you can give. Think about where you can give. Think of a giver. Think of Mother Teresa. Saint Teresa of Calcutta was an Albanian-Indian Roman Catholic nun and missionary (1910-1997). She said, "Spread love everywhere you go. Let no one ever come to you without leaving happier." What a legacy she left. She left all to follow Christ and to serve the poor people of India. It can be truly said of Mother Teresa that she allowed others to breathe easier because she lived.

She truly gave without expecting anything in return. Giving was her life. She was a living example of someone who concentrated on meeting the needs of others. We could be more like her. We can spread more happiness just by being a giver.

Let us work on being more giving. Giving of ourselves to others and for others without expecting anything in return, will give us, in return, a feeling of joy and proves we truly care. Think right now of someone in your life who you can help "breathe easier." I bet as you are thinking about that person, you are feeling happier already. Life, no matter what anybody says, is not just about getting. Instead of being selfish, let's make a more determined effort to be selfless.

Do NOW: Write down the names of people who you will give of yourself to. Write down what you will give them. You will be blessed.

Psychologist Jess Lair (1927-2000) once said, "Praise is like sunlight to the warm human spirit; we cannot flower and grow without it. And yet, while most of us are only too ready to apply to others the cold wind of criticism, we are somehow reluctant to give our fellow man the warm sunshine of praise."

Here's another quote. Charles Dickens, English writer and social critic (1812-1870) said, "No one is useless in this world who lightens the burdens of another." Let this attitude become part of your "bucket list". Make it a daily habit to carry the load of another.

How about that? Giving your "fellow man" praise. This can indeed *lighten the load* of others. It feels like the *warmth* of the sunshine. We **all** like that feeling, don't we? Think about giving someone "joy," "peace," "patience," "goodness," "kindness," "faithfulness," "love," "mercy," "gentleness," and "forgiveness." These are true and lasting gifts that you can give to others. If you haven't started giving these qualities away, start today.

You will be happier when you make others happier. Make a choice that everyone who comes into your presence will always leave happier. Distribute "blessed" feelings! Give people value. Keep yourself blessed by giving!

Think of someone you care about right now. Call them on the phone. Maybe send them an email or a text. Perhaps, even jot down a note and hand it to them when you see them. Some of you are waiting for others to give to you. That is not the way to approach life.

Hear this passage from **Philippians 2:3-4**. "*Do nothing out of selfish ambition or vain conceit, but in humility consider others better than yourselves.* Each of you should look not only to your own interests, but also to the interests of others." (New International Version)

As I write this, I am "giving" to my eighty-four-year-old mom, Dolly. I am looking out for her, as she is facing a serious medical challenge. I am helping her *breathe easier* by lending her a hand. I am blessed because I am able to do this.

One day while taking a walk around my mom's neighborhood, I stumbled upon a homeless woman behind a store. I asked her if I could pray for her. She said, "Yes, I always like prayers for me." After praying for her, I continued on my walk. Before returning back to my mom's apartment, I went by again and asked her if she needed anything. She mentioned she needed food. She only had a bag of Doritos. She also said she didn't have any clothes and needed a pair of shoes. I asked her what kind she was looking for. She said, "Tennis shoes."

Since, there was a thrift store right on the next corner, I went there and bought her some tennis shoes. Then coming back to my mom's place, I rounded up some food; soup, slices of cooked steak, some grapes, a banana, a couple of apples, and a bottle of water. I also gave her some paper plates and paper towels and a plastic spork and knife. During all this time, I felt a deep sense of gratitude for having this opportunity.

Also, since my mom had lost some weight, I was able to give the lady three tops and three pairs of pants.

It was a blessing to her. It didn't take much time out of my day.

Take this challenge today. Write down the names of all of your family members. Take some time and reflect on each one of them individually. Even if you are not currently talking to or getting along with all of them, still write their names down. As you write each name down, give yourself a minute or two and remember a "good" feeling of them from the past.

What qualities did I mention earlier? "Mercy" and "forgiveness." Apply these to your severed family relationships. Here's scripture I speak out over my family on a daily basis. It is adapted from **Colossians 3:13-15**:

> *My family is gentle and forbearing with one another, and if one has a difference (a grievance or complaint) against another, we readily pardon each other, even as the Lord has [freely] forgiven us, so must we also [forgive]. And above all these we [put on] love and enfold ourselves with the bond of perfectness [which binds everything together completely in ideal harmony]. And, we let the peace (soul harmony which comes) from Christ rule (act as umpire continually) in our hearts [deciding and settling with finality all questions that arise in our minds, in that peaceful state] to which as [members of Christ's] one body we were also called [to live]. And, we are thankful (appreciative), [giving praise to God always].*

From "The Secret Power of Speaking God's Word"
Joyce Meyer

Give of yourself. It's not hard to do.

Give of yourself. It's deep inside you.

Take a minute. Think and pray.

Focus on what you can DO or SAY

Giving of yourself will make life grand.

Just reach out. Lend a hand.

In doing so, you will find.

Peace in your heart and for your mind.

WHY I MUST GIVE OF MYSELF: Make a list of your reasons. **Do Now**.

COMPLETE THIS SENTENCE: Actions I can take to *give of myself* are...

Key #6   **Have Expectation**

"The one thing that will guarantee the successful conclusion of a doubtful undertaking is the faith in the beginning that we can do it."

William James

Choose to have expectation. How important is it to have expectation? It's very important because if you don't expect something, you usually won't get anything. This should make sense to you. Take a minute and think about that. What is something right now that you are expecting to get? If I were to ask you if you believed you are going to receive it, what would be your response? You would probably say, "Yes." That's exactly what I mean- believe and receive. Even the scriptures tell us, *"For assuredly, I say to you, whoever says to this mountain, 'Be removed and be cast into the sea,' and does not doubt in his heart, but believes that those things he says will be done, he will have whatever he says."* **Mark 11:23** (NKJV). Expectation is everything!

How do you know if you have expectation? You are persistent! We all know the story of Thomas Edison, American inventor and businessman, (1847-1931) who was the founder of the Edison Electric Light Company. Some of his inventions were the phonograph, the incandescent light bulb, and the motion picture camera. He had 1,000 failures before he had success at inventing the light bulb. But, what did he have? You guessed it. He had expectation. He persevered. He was confident he would have success if he just kept at it. This is what he said, "I have not failed. I've just found 10,000 ways that won't work."

If you don't have expectation or persistence, you won't keep going until you succeed. You will quit. You have to have faith at the start of your undertaking. At the very beginning of your "challenge," you have to have the hope and the belief that you will overcome and be able to do what you need to do. You prove you have this hope and belief by taking action. You develop attitudes and habits that will make sure you keep on keeping on. If you truly believe in yourself, you know that sooner or later, things will work out in your favor. Listen to this quote by Catherine of Siena, Italian philosopher and theologian, (1347-1380) "Nothing great was ever done without much enduring." You must focus on the final outcome. Minimize and limit distractions. A key aspect is to "see" the whole process and keep pressing forward.

Remember the children's story, *The Little Engine That Could*? This is an illustrated children's book, written by "Watty Piper," pen name for Arnold Munk, which was published in the year 1930, by Platt & Munk. The theme or message of this book is if you have optimism and work hard, you can be successful. This book is to give kids the belief that they can do what they put their minds to if they just keep trying and don't give up. In the story, the engine keeps repeating over and over, "I think I can!" "I think I can!"

Because of its expectation, this little blue engine was able to pull a long train of freight cars up a high hill and then go safely down. What an awesome theme for life. When I taught high school English, I didn't allow my students to use two phrases: "I can't", and "I'll try". No matter what issue or problem you are facing--a death in the family, sickness in your body, loss of a job, no money, anything at all--give yourself hope.

Do NOW: Say out loud, "I can!" "I have hope!" "I can make it!" In *Key #4*, I said you must use your imagination to see. Seeing is believing! In order to be it, you have to see it. In order to persevere, you must also be patient no matter how rough the way. Getting out of the situation is not the answer. You must trust the experience you're going through.

Remember to persevere. Figure out a way to keep on going. Keep expecting! Be courageous. Be competent. Be confident. Be tenacious and carry on! Life is not like a microwave oven. You can't just press a button, wait a minute, and be done. You can't rush through your issues and problems.

Become like a little child. Children expect and keep expecting, believing until they receive. I'm sure you've seen this. I have a granddaughter who will be a year old at the beginning of next month. When she wants a snack, she holds out her hand. She keeps on holding it out until she gets the snack. If she doesn't get it in an appropriate amount of time, or if she doesn't see some progress toward getting it, she makes a noise with her mouth. She has no doubt that sooner rather than later, she will get her snack if she keeps her hand out. Keep expecting. Keep *your hand* out. Believe you will receive.

If you don't have expectation, your life will be like this stanza:

> *If you think you are beaten, you are.*
>
> *If you think you dare not, you don't.*
>
> *If you like to win, but you think you can't,*
>
> *It is almost certain you won't.*
>
> Walter D. Wintle

Theodore Roosevelt, the 26th president of the United States, (1858-1919), once said, "Believe you can, and you're halfway there." Dale Brown, former men's head basketball coach at Louisiana State University writes in his book, *Words to Lift Your Spirits*, "When you've exhausted all possibilities, remember this, you haven't. The solution may only be in the next blow." Having expectation means you're optimistic. Not having expectation means you have no faith.

My nephew, Aiden, now thirteen, plays basketball. I had the opportunity to attend a few of his games while visiting in his home town. One particular game didn't start off too well for his team. They were behind by twenty points, and their momentum seemed slightly "off". As the game went on, slowly but surely, his team inched their way back into the lead. In fact, they won the game by seven points. The comeback was incredible! We all could hardly believe it! As I sat there watching the game unfold, I thought of this key: *having expectation*.

Although down by such a large amount, Aiden's team didn't allow the deficit to deter them from continuing to pursue the win. This is what expectation does. It pushes you to pursue the win, the goal, and the success regardless of the circumstances. We whooped and hollered! Then, we went out and ate to celebrate!

An excellent way to cultivate expectation is to think about your mission and your values. Along with your mission and values comes a set of goals. We will talk a little bit more about goals in *Key #9 Purpose to Live*. I'm sure most people know who Sylvester Stallone is, star of Rocky, Rambo, and the Expendables, just to name a few. Stallone is a person who had expectations and never gave up faith. Stallone refused to take "no" for an answer, even when he was down to his last hundred dollars and sleeping in his car. He persevered. He kept his optimism. In the end, his optimism and expectation paid off. He starred in the movie he wrote, *Rocky,* which garnered critical acclaim, and his successful career was born.

A mission and values are something you stand for and stand up for. Every day, when you wake, have a mission, something that defines you. Being mission-minded—having a driving force-can be a catalyst for your life expectations. Additionally, a set of values will determine how you live and why you live.

What is your mission statement? What are your values? What is your purpose? Your mission is what "matters" to you and your desires or life's intentions.

Do Now: Write a statement which declares your intentions for your life. How are you going to live your life and who are you going to affect?

Don't let go of your optimism! No matter the pressures of the world or the pressures in your life, believe now that you will make it through. Say, "I'm not beaten!" Keep going and remember life is an endurance race. How we think determines how we live. If we want a different outcome, we must think in a different way. If you want to *be* a different way, *think* a different way. It's that simple! That's how you persevere.

Get into the "habit" of believing! Wake up in the morning and say to yourself, "I BELIEVE!" "I AM WINNING!" You must be purposeful and diligent. You can do it!

WHY I MUST HAVE EXPECTATION: List your reasons **now.**

COMPLETE THIS SENTENCE: Actions I can take to *have expectation* are:

Key #7   Appreciate Life

"Appreciate life even if it's not perfect. Happiness is not fulfillment of what we wish for but an appreciation of what we have."

picturequotes.com

Choose to appreciate life. Why? It is the only one you're going to get. Even as you're reading this book, your life's clock is ticking. Appreciating your life or appreciating it more is crucial, and you must start now. I know sometimes you don't always like your life's circumstances, but you are still alive. Your circumstances can change. Decide to take and "see" life one day at a time. Don't try to figure out everything all the time. Just go with the flow!

    Don't take life for granted. I almost died last week! At least, that's what my husband thought I was doing—dying. In his words, *I was pale. My eyes were rolling back inside of my head, and I barely had a pulse.* He was scared! Well, as you can see, I made it. I'm still writing this book. As I grow older, I realize how short my time on this earth really is. My life could have ended in that bathtub.

    Appreciating life is something we must all do. How do we appreciate life? We appreciate life, by first, being thankful that we have life. Next, we appreciate our life by taking the time to enjoy our life day by day, hour by hour, and minute by minute. We can't let our life slip away. We have to savor each moment.

Appreciating life should be, as they say, a "no brainer". It shouldn't be something we even have to think about. It should come naturally. No matter what is going on, we should be grateful. Just last week, when my husband thought I was dying, my life flashed before me, but I was given mercy. I am grateful and truly appreciate that I'm alive. Life is a precious thing, and we should not waste it being ungrateful.

To be truly happy, you must live in today, in the present. Ask yourself if you appreciate life or just tolerate it. If you murmur or complain, are negative, feel bored most of the time, have a scowl on your face, don't "feel" like doing much, and get impatient or upset easily, you are tolerating life not enjoying it. People who tolerate life are usually scornful. People who just tolerate life are hard to be around. They are not very grateful and look for the "bad" in everything.

Do NOW: Stop and jot down three things you are grateful for. Then, write down why you are grateful for them. I bet there is someone who would like to trade places with you.

1.

2.

3.

You need to realize that not all things in your life can change. Instead of worrying for those things you cannot change, focus on accepting the things in your life that are good, the things you have. You can accomplish this by appreciating the small things – the smile of a child, the touch of a hand, the smell of the rain, the taste of your favorite food, the sound of a church choir singing to the Lord. So, you see, you are blessed with something so simple as your senses, but that blessing is no small matter.

Write it down. If you are having a hard time appreciating your life, reflect, meditate, or pray until you are able to get yourself in a better state of mind. Appreciating your life is vital if you are to be a happy person. Think about what you have right now that you appreciate and write it down.

Here's a secret. There is no perfect life. You could be dead. Life is to be lived. Look at my dad. He is a young, cool, eighty-seven-year old "walking ball" of energy. He doesn't let anything stop him! When he walks into a room, everyone turns around to look at who just walked in. First of all, he is dressed immaculately from head to toe, from his hat all the way down to his shoes. Secondly, he has a large smile on his face and simply exudes joy.

He has the secret to appreciating life. His life is far from perfect, but he knows how to live it as though it was. He is an inspiration to us all. My dad has overcome various medical issues and is healthier now than he has ever been. He cooks, does art, exercises, takes piano lessons, works in a senior center part-time, and is a faithful church-goer.

We all have some sort of problem or issue in our lives. There will constantly be at least one thing "hanging over our heads" so to speak. We **all** have a cross to bear. So, what? If you are still having a difficult time coming up with at least one thing you are appreciative for, think harder!

In order to really appreciate life, you must fight discouragement. Hear these words by G.K. Chesterton, English writer, poet, and philosopher, (1874-1936), "Hope is the power of being cheerful in circumstances which we know to be desperate." Scripture says, *"Be joyful in hope, patient in affliction, faithful in prayer."* **Romans 12:12**. (NIV).

Hope is vital! You cannot have an appreciation for life if you feel hopeless. You have to maintain a sense of joy. Even in trying times, fix your mind on believing in a better life than you are experiencing right now. "See" God as bigger than your problems. Be patient.
How about this? Do a MIND MAKEOVER!

Make a list: On one side put Negatives. On the other side put Positives. Here's a challenge for you. Keep writing down things until your "positives" list outranks your "negatives" list. By doing this, you will see and experience progress. It will help you to think on the "good" and limit your obsession with the "bad".

It's very important for you to realize you don't have to be where you want to be in life to have appreciation for your life or to be happy. Just imagine where you could be next month or next year if you can only start to live life truly in a joyful, appreciative state today. French poet Guillaume Apollinaire (1880-1918) once said, "Now and then it's good to pause in our pursuit of happiness and just be happy."

Do your utmost to live life fully! Appreciating life means appreciating your family, your spouse, your children, your relatives, your health, your strength, your work, your body, and your mind. It means appreciating your ability to reason, to talk, to imagine, and even to laugh. These are all things to enjoy. We, as a whole, have got to stop dwelling so much on what is going wrong and focus more on what is going right!

Here's how to focus on what is going right. In the morning before you get out of bed, think of at least three things you are thankful for and speak them out loud, i.e., "I am thankful for:"

1.

2.

3.

By doing this exercise, you will indeed feel more thankful and blessed.

"A good life is when you assume nothing, do more, need less, smile often, dream big, laugh a lot, and realize how blessed you are." Zig Ziglar, American author, (1926-2012). I LOVE this quote! It mainly says to me to live and NOT WORRY.

A great life is waiting for you! Don't settle for anything less. There is a highly publicized poem written by David L. Weatherford, entitled, "Slow Dance." The refrain is this: *You better slow down, don't dance so fast, time is short, the music won't last.* The poem goes on to say and ends with the line; *Life is not a race, so take it slower, hear the music before your song is over.*

What did that last line say? *Before your song is over.* A few years ago, a friend of mine went into heart surgery, and he never came out. He had no idea his "song" was about to be over. Truth be told, you have no idea when yours is over either. Here's another suggestion. Get a journal or notebook and think of five people you appreciate. After writing their names down, call them or write them-- text or email—and let them know how much you appreciate them, are thankful for them, and why. Or, just go visit them!

Remember, "Happiness is an appreciation of what you have, not the fulfillment of what you wish for." Also, life is NOT PERFECT! You will be happier living day by day.

And, daily, perhaps as you are about to lie down for the night, tell yourself what you appreciated about the day you just spent in the land of the living. Watch your attitude and life change for the better.

WHY I MUST APPRECIATE LIFE: List as many reasons as you can.

COMPLETE THIS SENTENCE: Actions I can take to *appreciate life* are…

Key #8 Permit Mistakes

"Freedom is not worth having if it does not include the freedom to make mistakes."

Mahatma Gandhi

Choose to permit mistakes. Lots of them! Why? Because we are human beings--not robots. As humans, we are prone to making mistakes. In fact, we wouldn't be human if we didn't make mistakes. We'd be God!

You have to allow yourself to make mistakes without getting "down in the dumps" about it. Why do so many of us become ill-at-ease and unhappy when things are not going well? It's simply because we are not making allowances for our blunders. In the last chapter, I said there is no perfect life. It is time for us to stop putting ourselves down for the many mistakes we make daily and for the numerous mistakes we've already made in our lives. If I made a list of all of the mistakes I have made, it would probably fill a volume. Even if you feel you have made a total "mess" of your life and mistake after mistake, it's okay. Forget about it! Forgive yourself!

Give yourself permission to make mistakes. We are too hard on ourselves. Our happiness or unhappiness can't be based on our performance. We can't kick ourselves when we're down. Just because you fail, doesn't mean you're a failure. Here's another quote by John Wooden, "Success is never final. Failure is never fatal. It's courage that counts." With every mistake, you still have a chance to rebound!

The key is not to allow your mistakes to cause you to quit or give up. You never have to be beaten. In a race, if you fall, you just need to get back up and keep going. The same goes in life— if you fall, you just need to get back up and keep going! Learn from your mistakes and persevere through them.

My son, Tim, had to do that. He had to "get back up". His challenge was the California Bar Exam. It was a tough challenge. But, he learned from his mistakes, persevered, and received his license. He knew he had to keep driving himself forward for himself and his family. It took a few tries, but he was successful. He knew it was only God that gave him the ability to pick himself back up when he fell and push through to victory. The day we heard the news he passed the test was a great day!

All of your mistakes are in the past, behind you. Philippians 3:13 says, "...; *but one thing I do, forgetting those things which are behind and reaching forward to those things which are ahead*," (NKJV). Your mistakes, no matter how recent, are in the past and forgetting them is the key to moving forward—to having and pursuing the ability to be happy. Why is this so hard for many of us to do? It is hard for most people to do because we are not reaching ahead. Going over and over what has already happened leaves us no time to dream, plan, or contemplate our future. "Don't waste your time looking back on what you've lost. Move on, for life is not meant to be traveled backwards." Unknown

The only way to unlock joy is to go after something. We must diligently reach forward to what's ahead. We must PRESS ON! It is up to us. We can let our mistakes and our failures keep us down and defeated, or we can press on like my son, Tim. And, remember this, "If you're making mistakes, it means you're out there doing something." Neil Gaiman, English author. AMEN!

Another key is do not beat yourself up. Don't dwell too much on the mistake. Do your best not to become depressed in the process. Take some time to de-stress. What are some ways you can do that? Take a breather, literally. Take some deep breaths. Sit down for a minute. Clear your mind. Meditate on something good. Pray. Sing a praise melody. Take a nap. Remember Key #2 *Energize Your Soul*? Here is another area to *Stop, Look, and Listen!*

Guess what I did the other day? I locked myself out of the house. I had decided to go for a walk. Unbeknownst to me, I had taken the wrong house key. Everything was just honky dory until I got back home, attempted to unlock the door, and realized I had the wrong key. Amazing! And, you know I had a million things to do and get done. Oh, well. I started thinking about what to do. I was still wearing my exercise clothes. I had no phone, no money, nothing. I was able to get into the back yard through the side gate and sit in the hammock we have. I sat there for about two hours.

Did I moan? No. What good would that have done? Eventually, I went across the street and had my neighbor call my son to come and help me. I was super glad it was a cool day. It was nice being outside. While I sat in the hammock, after I stopped trippin' that I had the wrong key, I began to sing songs. I voiced praises to the Lord. I napped. I meditated. You know what I didn't do? I didn't let it ruin my day. I didn't beat myself up over a mistake.

I would say that, really, this mistake helped me learn. It helped me learn to make sure I have a phone with me at all times. It helped me learn to slow down long enough to ensure I have the right keys. This was an inconvenience, for sure. It wasn't planned and could have been avoided. But, I kept my joy. We can and should let every mistake or obstacle be a learning event. Everything in life is not going to go easy or be easy. That's why permitting mistakes is important.

Living an overcoming life where we can keep "joy" everyday no matter what happens will be a reality when we learn to truly let every obstacle be a learning event. We have to continue to work on our life, believing that all things— mistakes included- work together for our good. . What did Gandhi's quote at the beginning of the chapter say? Freedom is NOT worth having if you can't make mistakes! Think about that.

How many mistakes have you made in your life? Because I know I have made too many to count. So,

TODAY, pick yourself up and have the courage to forgive yourself, to learn from your mistakes, and to press on. Don't be passive. Don't hesitate to take any action simply because you feel you will fail or make a mistake. How can you ever enjoy life if you can't be patient with yourself or are overly critical? You are an imperfect being; we *all* are. Be patient. Be constructive. Be forgiving! Never forget that.

Give yourself *grace*. Even if you "bite off" more than you can chew, swallow what you can. Tomorrow is another day. You can begin again or adjust some things. There is a God, and He allows second chances. So, you messed up. Haven't we all? Keep striving even though life may strike you down. You are only "out" if you stay down.

Don't worry over your past mistakes. I know this is easier said than done. Here's a tactic for you.

Do NOW: Make a list of your past mistakes on a separate sheet of paper. Don't stress out over this. You don't need to list them all. Besides, you probably won't even remember them all. Once you have written out the list, read over it, and then tear it up! Throw the pieces in the trash or burn them up!

Concentrate on your strengths not your weaknesses. We will all have bad days. Keep a good outlook. Even with all of your mistakes, don't give up on you! Talk good about yourself. Let God speak to you. He knows your heart. Look at where God has brought you. Look at and focus on the things you have accomplished.

Do NOW: Write down some things you have done or accomplished this past week.

WHY I MUST PERMIT MISTAKES: Write down your reasons **now**.

COMPLETE THIS SENTENCE: Actions I can take to *permit mistakes* are…

Key #9   Purpose to Live

"Believe in your heart that you're meant to live a life full of passion, purpose, magic, and miracles."

Roy T. Bennett

Choose to purpose to live. Choose to live a purposeful life. Why? You need a purpose to live, a reason to wake up every morning. You also need to be purposeful about your purpose, that is, you need to "be about it". When you get down to it, you would not even be on this planet right now if you did not have a purpose. In my last book, *BEING DETERMINED: How to be Relentless in Pursuing Your Dreams in 15 Simple Ways*, I talked about ways to go about your purpose-- to fulfill your dreams. It is never too late to discover your purpose.

    Do NOW: Jot down some things you like or some things that bring you joy. These could be a part of your purpose. What things have you already gone through that could be a part of your purpose? Listen to this, "Just because the past didn't turn out like you wanted it to, doesn't mean the future can't be better than you ever imagined." Ziad K. Abdelnour, Lebanese, American author. Exactly! Anyway, none of us has an unblemished past. Let's just discover anew how we can be useful and bring value today.

Living your life with a purpose will enable you to focus and finish. You will see your life as a race you are running to win. Having a purpose to live means you will look for, recognize, and seize opportunities when they arise. Having a purpose means you won't just see problems as being insurmountable. You will look for ways to find answers to your problems. Henry David Thoreau, American essayist, poet, philosopher, and abolitionist, and historian (1817-1862), once said, "It's not what you look at that matters, it's what you see."

Having a purpose means you will have goals. Goals will keep you going and advancing in the right direction. Have at least one goal. Write down your goal and work toward it daily. You might be surprised to know that just having a goal you are working toward can bring a sense of well-being and happiness. "See" something that you can work toward.

What's your purpose now?

What is important for you to do now?

Take a minute and write it down. Whatever it is, choose today to begin. Keep finding a purpose to live. Think about how it is to ride a bicycle. Former U.S. Representative, Claude D. Pepper (1900-1989), once said, "Life is like riding a bicycle. You don't fall off until you stop pedaling." Don't stop moving toward your purpose once you begin. In other words, never stop pedaling! It's your daily effort that supplies the power to keep yourself moving forward.

Do NOW: Make a list of one monthly goal for each of the next six months. Place this list where you can see it and refer to it every day.

Writing gives me a purpose. I write a monthly email inspirational newsletter entitled, "Almond Joy." I love to motivate and inspire others to excel. This is my calling. This is my purpose. I also give motivational and inspirational talks to various groups, clubs, schools, etc. Having a purpose gives me overflowing joy and will give you overflowing joy in everyday living as well. Purposeless living is not living at all. Without any purpose or goal, your life will be aimless and drifting nowhere. You need a plan. You need a blueprint. You need a list. You need some kind of organization. You can't just live randomly. That won't work.

Here's a thought for you: "Purpose is what gives life a meaning...a drifting boat always drifts downstream." This quote is attributed to American clergyman and social reformer, Charles H. Parkhurst, (1842-1933). Wow! Amazing, huh? What is this quote telling you? Don't drift downstream. Rise up! Get up and get something done, TODAY. Have a purpose.

Many years ago, at a sales convention I attended, one of the conference speakers made this comment, "Even a brick wants to be something." How cool is that? I always remember that statement. Let me repeat it. Even a brick wants to be something! You want to be something. You want to do something important. All it takes is you finally deciding to do what you have been designed to do. I often tell my audiences to think of something they would do even if they didn't get paid for it. That is probably your passion. Writing, speaking, and singing are my passions. You would never have to pay me to do them.

A great movie, *Chariots of Fire*, released in the year, 1981, was based on the true story of two British athletes, Eric Liddell and Harold Abrahams, during the 1924 Olympics in Paris, France. Liddell is a Christian and Abrahams is Jewish. They both experience various hardships and challenges which made this telling of their story remarkable. Eric wouldn't race on a Sunday, and Harold faced the sting of anti-Semitism.

What is so great about this movie is its inspiration. No matter their obstacles and problems, both knew and felt running was their purpose. Eric Liddell even said, "I believe that God made me for a purpose. But, He also made me fast, and when I run, I feel His pleasure." He also says in the film that *the will to win comes from within*. Your will to win will come from inside you. For Liddell his purpose was fulfilled. He won *gold* and was ready to return to missionary work in China—the other purpose God had given to him.

Magic and miracles. Do you want a life filled with these? Here's some great news for you! If you look, you will find. **Matthew 7:7** (NKJV) says, *"Ask, and it will be given to you; seek, and you will find; knock, and it will be opened to you."* John Lubbock, an English politician, (1928-2016) said, "What we see depends mainly on what we look for." What are you looking for, and what are you seeing? What did I say in the first paragraph? BE ABOUT IT! Take the time you have and use it wisely. Be a good steward. Don't be careless. Ask. Seek. Knock.

Like Eric Liddell and Harold Abrahams, find something you love and do well, and keep doing it!

Don't say you're too old, either. What is age but a number? I read this on a poster, "Attitude more than age determines ability." If you are determined to have a purpose for living, you will find one regardless of your age. My challenge to you is to persevere through whatever obstacles or issues you may be facing. You only fail if you quit! With a purpose, some patience, perseverance, and prayer you can make it!

Look at Noah. Do you remember his story? Noah and the Ark. It's in the book of *Genesis, Chapters 6-9*. Noah was building an ark for his family and animals to be saved because of a flood that was coming upon the earth. Now, up to this point, it had never even rained down upon the earth. But, Noah was given a mandate to build it. This became his purpose, his calling. Regardless of the obstacles and negativity he faced, he had faith and believed God.

As stated in **Hebrews 11:7**, "*By faith, Noah being divinely warned of things not yet seen …prepared an ark…and became heir of the righteousness which is according to faith.*" (NKJV). He was diligent, steadfast, purposeful, and faithful. You must be the same. You must make progress toward your purpose, daily, by having faith and hope. Believe in the destiny that awaits you.

Here's another suggestion for you to think and do. Get a "theme" for your life. What does your life stand for? What message is your life conveying? Seriously, think about what your life stands for and what your life message is. The theme for my life is: *To Persist*!

Your purpose is to _____

Write down your life's theme. *You will* persist if you have a purpose. *You will* finish your tasks. *You will* have determination. *You will* see it through. You won't let anything deter you from *asking, seeking,* and *knocking* until the way is opened up for you. You won't settle for mediocrity. Even when things are not looking so great, *you will* hang in there! The late president, Franklin D. Roosevelt, (1882-1945) once said, "When you reach the end of your rope, tie a knot in it and hang on."

How well do you know yourself? At the beginning of this book in *Key #1*, I talked about how vital it is to "be yourself". The more you know yourself and are yourself, the more you can know and fulfill your purpose--the more you can finish what you start. Keep a good attitude, and you won't be defeated. Don't be discouraged. Magic and miracles are on their way. Hang on!!

Say now, "I'm a finisher!"

Remember to ask yourself, "What am I looking for?" "What am I seeing?"

WHY I MUST PURPOSE TO LIVE: Make a list of your reasons.

COMPLETE THIS SENTENCE: Actions that I can take to *purpose to live* are...

Key #10 Yearn for the Best

"Always try to do your best. Never give up, and God will take care of everything else."

Dale Brown

Choose to yearn for the best! Why would you want to do that? It wouldn't be too wise to yearn for the worst now, would it? You know how ridiculous that sounds. It's the "best" that we **all** want. No one wants to live a ho-hum life. How boring would that be? That would be no fun and bring no lasting happiness. Bored people are unhappy people. When I taught English, I told my students to be the best and give it their best. For the most part, they did that! Except for a few "party poopers," most of the students bought into my "crazy" love of teaching.

Have a belief that the best is yet to come, your best career, your best health, your best family. It's time to take control of your life and your happiness. You get out of life what you put into it. Yearn for the best, and you will DO your best, BE your best, and STRIVE for the best! It all boils down to attitude and persistence. This is a daily process. You can't wake up one morning and decide not to yearn for the best.

Remember, you only have this one life to live, so live it well. You will be happier and more content if you give this life your best shot! Grab ahold of your abundant, overflowing life. Do it NOW! Let everyday be a time to unlock and find joy. Live your life wholeheartedly not half-heartedly. There's an old, Negro, spiritual song that goes like this: "Lord, I'm runnin,' tryin' to make a hundred 'cause ninety-nine and a half just won't do!"

Give your life today and every day, 100%. We must be ALL IN! Aristotle, an ancient Greek philosopher and scientist, (384 BC-322 BC) once said, "We are what we repeatedly do. Excellence, therefore, is not an act but a habit." Living your best, excellent life must become a habit.

Find something that brings you joy! I heard a song the other day on YOUTUBE. The song was "Better" by Hezekiah Walker, a gospel music artist and pastor. His song communicates a message that things will get better because God is in control. Believing this message will surely free you!

No matter what state you are presently in, you must never give up. You can NEVER quit! Things will get better. You must trust and believe God will make it better. **Isaiah 41:10** tells us, "*So do not fear, for I am with you; do not be dismayed, for I am your God. I will strengthen you and help you; I will uphold you with my righteous right hand.*" (NIV) Even if you are having a rough day today, even if you are crying inside today, look for something good today. Remember, GOD IS IN CONTROL, and it will get better.

You must also be disciplined. Listen to this quote by author, Maya Angelou, "Someone was hurt before you, wronged before you, hungry before you, frightened before you, beaten before you, humiliated before you, raped before you….yet somehow survived…..You can do anything you choose to do." *Anything you choose to do*, but you MUST choose to do SOMETHING! You cannot wait to "yearn for the best". You have to yearn for the best today! You must not rely on feelings alone. Whether you feel like it or not, you want your life to be excellent. This requires willpower. Willpower will help you live life based less on your "up" and "down" emotions. You can do and be your BEST because you choose to.

To yearn for the best, you must claim the victory now! You must keep yourself in a state of trust. As you come to the end of this book, think of your life as an audition. In auditions, you have one shot! There are no do-overs. If your life is going to be the best it can be, it's now or never.

What did Dale Brown, former college basketball coach at Louisiana State University say? *God will take care of everything else*. This should be a comfort to you and compel you to strive to do your best. What have you got to lose? It's really pretty simple, isn't it? Don't allow your brain or thoughts to complicate your life. Live and leave the rest in God's hands. It boils down to faith! That's what it takes, really.

Believe you can have the best. Don't talk yourself out of it! If you want to have the best, you will. Let this be your truth. A life based on the truth is a life of happiness. **John 8:32** says, *"And you shall know the truth, and the truth shall make you free."* (NKJV) Don't let any issues from your past continue to hinder you or stop you from living your best life. In *Key #8*, we talked about permitting mistakes. This is why permitting mistakes is so important. You can't be defined by your past. In regard to your past mistakes, remember: "It was just a lesson, not a life sentence." *Power of Positivity*

AMEN! Get yourself out of your self-imposed prison cell. Take your chains off! Choose the best and get the best.

Do NOW:

Tell yourself, "I live my best life!" I had to tell myself that. I tell myself this daily. Regardless of how my flesh feels or what I think, if negative, I choose to live above what I may "feel". I am in charge of what I think. I can choose what I think. For me, as a Christian, I live by the Holy Scripture, which is the Word of God. If God tells me I can, then I can. He tells me in **Philippians 4:13**, *"I can do all things through Christ who strengthens me."* (NKJV) I believe that. You can believe that.

Here's another quote by the late inspirational author and speaker, Zig Ziglar, "Positive thinking won't let you do anything. But, it will let you do everything better than negative thinking will." Let's face it! Being negative or having negativity sucks! Remember an earlier quote at the beginning of *Key #4 Nourish Your Mind*? *As you think in your heart, so you are.* If you think you will never have the best, you most likely won't. Thinking negatively gets you more of the same. Here's another saying by Eckhart Tolle. "If you get the inside right, the outside will fall into place." How easy is this? It may not be easy, but it is doable.

Truth be told this might be a life-long process. Daily work on getting your mind right, so your life will be right. I would suggest you give yourself more love and more forgiveness. Yearning for your best will mean releasing yourself from past hurts and entanglements. Believe in your gut that you can do it!

If you want happiness, you can have it! You control your happiness. Make sure you don't just try to be happy. If you are only trying, you are not resting on God and His promises. Furthermore, trying isn't believing. Anything or any quality you want or desire to have has to be activated by faith and belief. You must speak good words over yourself and over your life! "Whatever we plant in our subconscious mind and nourish with repetition and emotion, will one day become a reality," Earl Nightingale, American radio speaker and author, (1921-1989).

Be careful what you plant. Why? Because what you plant is coming up and out. For overflowing joy in everyday living, happiness has to be planted. Whether you want it to or not, your reality will come. Make it a good one.

This life is to be lived to its fullest. We are also told in the scriptures that Jesus came to give us an abundant, overflowing life. So, yes, we can have this kind of life. **John 10:10b**, *"I have come that they may have life, and that they may have it more abundantly."* (NKJV). John Assaraf of NeuroGym has designed what is called an "exceptional life blueprint." This blueprint causes you to focus on your life's purpose, mission, top goals, habits, daily rituals, etc.

JohnAssaraf@myneurogym.com. Reading my blueprint daily reminds me to focus on living my "best" life by daily focusing on my habits, my goals, my growth, and my contribution.

Ask yourself if you're yearning. ***Ask yourself*** if you're longing, desiring, wanting, wishing, hankering, hungering, thirsting, etc. Go for the gusto! *Gusto* means "with vigor, enthusiasm, relish, enjoyment, delight, glee, pleasure, satisfaction, zest, spirit, and fervor". ***Ask yourself*** if there has ever been a time in your life when you had these tendencies. When was it? What was it for? If you had it, when did you lose it? How? Did you let something, someone, or some happening steal your joy? By doing this exercise, it will help you conjure up how to go for the "gusto" **now**!

Close your eyes and count to ten. Now, take a deep breath. *Be Happy!* It's your divine right and your choice to make. You are the one who must claim, proclaim, and declare your birthright. Every day is a new day to declare your happiness. Every day is a new day to "kick sadness to the curb". Don't just wake up and hurry into your day. Take time to develop your "happiness stance!" What is a happiness stance?

Happiness stance:

Today, I declare and decree a magnificent day! I believe all good and perfect gifts are coming to me, today. Goodness is abounding to me and mercy is following me. I am joyful today! My past is behind me. My future is new and unfolding. Doors of opportunity are opening up for me today. I "see" things anew. Every step I take today leads me closer to my best life.

WHY I MUST YEARN FOR THE BEST: List your reasons **now**.

COMPLETE THIS SENTENCE: Actions that I can take to *yearn for the best* are....

Prayer for Happiness:

Dear heavenly Father,

    I come to You now, and I thank You for all the blessings You have given me, especially my life. I ask You to keep my mind open to all that is available for me this day.

    Forgive me for focusing on all that is wrong with my life instead of on all that is right. I give You my heart and life today to direct me according to Your plans.

Thank You, heavenly Father,

Amen!

Thanks again for taking another journey with me. Our journey for happiness. This has been a great journey!

CLAIM YOUR BIRTHRIGHT!

Remember, "a peaceful heart is a happy heart".".

"To be happy, a man must first know what happiness is," Jean Jacques Rousseau, Genevan philosopher, (1712-1778).

As you read my book; hopefully, you garnered thoughts, ideas, and suggestions to assist you in your daily quest to have an overcoming, joy-filled life.

To your lasting happiness,

Janice Almond

OTHER BOOKS:

BEING GRATEFUL: How to Open the Door to a More Fulfilled & Abundant Life in 13 Easy Steps

BEING DETERMINED: How to be Relentless in Pursuing Your Dreams in 15 Simple Ways

Connect with me at: www.janicealmondbooks.com

https:// twitter.com/janicealmondjoy

www.facebook.com/lifeisonlywhatyoumakeit

"Be Joyful Always!"
1 Thess. 5:18

ABOUT THE AUTHOR

Janice is an inspirational writer, speaker, and book publisher. She is a former high school English teacher, First Lady in ministry, and community college professor.

She's had the privilege of traveling around Europe, joining Toastmasters, and receiving a B.A. degree in Communication Studies from UCLA during the John Wooden basketball years (1970's). Later, she earned two Master's degrees in Education, Multicultural Education and Educational Administration.

She currently resides in California with her husband of more than forty years, David Almond. Her hope is that her works inspire, uplift, and encourage you to fulfill your full potential, and to live a life of purpose.

She conducts BEING GRATEFUL & BEING DETERMINED Workshops. For speaking engagements or workshops, please contact her at:

ZION Publishing House
P.O. Box 3522
Riverside, Ca.92519
(928) 234-6159
Email:janicealmondbooks@gmail.com
www.janicealmondbooks.com

About ZION Publishing House

ZION Publishing House is a family-owned publishing company based in Southern California and Washington, DC. ZION helps Christian authors tell their stories by providing an affordable alternative to traditional publishing. Our mission is to maintain a platform that educates and empowers independent Christian authors. We do this by cultivating talent in the inspirational and self-help genres for novice and experienced authors. The path to publishing can be daunting and extremely complex. We take pride in taking our clients by the hand and walking them through the publishing process to ensure they not only have a high-quality product that resonates with the reader, but they understand the many facets of the publishing industry and what it means to be a published author.

If you are a writer looking for an affordable path to publishing, visit our website at www.zionpublishinghouse.com to learn more.

NOTES

NOTES

NOTES

NOTES

NOTES

NOTES

NOTES

NOTES

NOTES

NOTES

NOTES

NOTES

NOTES

NOTES

NOTES

www.ingramcontent.com/pod-product-compliance
Lightning Source LLC
Chambersburg PA
CBHW030452010526
44118CB00011B/892